Animal Dictionary

BY JANE WERNER WATSON
PICTURES BY FEODOR ROJANKOVSKY

GOLDEN PRESS
Western Publishing Company, Inc.
Racine, Wisconsin

The ANIMAL DICTIONARY will help young children to explore the animal kingdom. Arranged in alphabetical order are many familiar animals, as well as some that will be strange to young readers. The definitions by Jane Werner Watson are short and simple, and each animal is illustrated in color by Feodor Rojankovsky, long famous for his pictures of animals. Thus younger children will find this a fascinating picture book, and older ones will learn how to use a first, very simple dictionary.

Fourth Printing, 1972

© 1960 by Western Publishing Company, Inc.
All rights reserved. Produced in U.S.A.

GOLDEN, A LITTLE GOLDEN BOOK®, and GOLDEN PRESS®
are trademarks of Western Publishing Company, Inc.

A

alligator

The alligator lives near water.

angelfish

Angelfish are bright-colored.

animal

An animal is a living thing that moves about.

ant

Ants are hard-working insects.

anteater

The anteater has a long nose. It eats ants with its tongue.

antelope

The antelope is a graceful deer.

ape

An ape is a kind of monkey.

armadillo

The armadillo wears scales.

B

baboon
A baboon is a monkey which lives on the ground.

badger
The badger digs a burrow for its home.

bass

Bass are fish.
There are many kinds of bass.

bat
Bats look like mice with wings.
They fly at night.

bear

The bear eats fish, bugs, roots and berries. It likes honey, too.

beaver

Beavers build dams across streams.

bee
Bees are busy insects. They make honey.

beetle

The beetle is an insect with a hard shell.

bird

Birds have feathers and can fly.

bluejay

The bluejay is a noisy bird and sometimes steals eggs.

bobcat

The bobcat is an American wild cat.

buffalo

Buffalo live on the open prairie.

bug

Bugs are insects with wings.

burrow

A burrow is an animal's underground home.

butterfly

The butterfly has pretty wings.

C

calf

A calf is a young cow.

camel

The camel stores food in its hump. It has padded feet for walking on sand.

cardinal

The father cardinal is a beautiful red songbird.

cat

A cat has soft fur and sharp claws. There are many kinds of cats.

caterpillar

Caterpillars grow into butterflies or moths.

cattle

Cows and oxen are cattle.

centipede

Centipede means "hundred-footed." A centipede has many pairs of legs.

chameleon

A chameleon is a lizard. It can change color.

chicken

Chickens live on farms.
Their eggs are good to eat.

chimpanzee

Chimpanzees can learn
to do many things.

chinchilla

The chinchilla has very soft,
beautiful fur.

chipmunk

Chipmunks are small, lively cousins
of the squirrel.

clam

A clam lives between two shells.
Its home is at the bottom of the sea.

claw

Claws are long, sharp nails.

cocoon

A caterpillar
spins a cocoon around itself.

condor

A condor is a very large
American bird.

coral

Coral is made of tiny sea animals' shells.

cormorant

Cormorants are birds that catch fish. Sometimes they dive deep under water.

cow

Cows give milk which we drink.

coyotes

Coyotes howl at night. They are also called prairie wolves.

crab

Crabs wear shells and walk sideways.

crane

A crane is a long-legged wading bird.

cricket

Crickets hop and chirp.

crocodile

The crocodile is a big reptile. It lives near water.

D

deer

Father deer are stags.
They have antlers.
Mother deer are called does.

dinosaur

Dinosaurs were huge animals.
They lived long ages ago.

dogs

Dogs are friendly animals.

dove

A dove is a gentle bird
that makes a cooing noise.

dragonfly

The dragonfly has two sets
of shiny wings.

duck

The duck is a bird
that likes to swim.
It lives near water.

E

eagle
The big eagle hunts by day.

eel
The eel is a long, thin fish.

egg
Baby birds and fish hatch from eggs.

elephant
The elephant is very strong.
Sometimes it works for people.

elk
The elk is a big deer.
It looks a little like
its cousin the moose.

F

fawn
A fawn
is a baby deer.

feathers
Birds have feathers.

firefly
Fireflies
can glow
at night.

fish
Fish live in water.

flamingo

The flamingo is a bird. It has long legs and a long neck.

fledgling

Fledglings are baby birds. They have not yet learned to fly.

flippers

Some animals have flippers to help them swim.

fly

A fly is a buzzing, two-winged insect.

fox

The fox has a long, bushy tail.

frog

Frogs live near water.

Gila monster

The Gila monster is a poisonous lizard. Its name is pronounced "heel-a."

G goose

A goose is a long-necked bird.

gorilla
The gorilla is the biggest of the apes.

grasshopper

Grasshoppers can leap high.

grub

Grubs are insect babies.

gull
Gulls live near water and eat fish.

H

hawk

A hawk is a hunting bird.

hedgehog

The hedgehog is a prickly insect-eater. It lives in Europe.

heron

The heron is a tall bird that lives near water.

hippopotamus
The hippopotamus lives in lakes and rivers in Africa.

hoof
A hoof is a horny covering on an animal's foot.

horn

Cattle and deer have horns on their heads.

horse

Horses are strong and run very fast.

hound

A hound is a hunting dog.

hummingbird

The tiny hummingbird flies very fast.

I J

insect

Insects have six legs and two pairs of wings.

jackal

The jackal is a wild dog.

jack rabbit

The jack rabbit can take long jumps.

jaguar

The jaguar is a fierce wild cat.

jellyfish

Jellyfish are soft, jelly-like sea animals.

K

kangaroo

A mother kangaroo carries its baby in a pouch.

katydid

The katydid makes a sound like its name.

kingfisher

The kingfisher eats fish and insects.

kitten

A kitten is a baby cat.

koala

Koalas live in Australian gum trees.

L

ladybug

The ladybug is a pretty little beetle.

lamb

A lamb is a baby sheep.

larva

A larva is the young of an insect.

leafhopper

Leafhoppers often eat farmers' crops.

lemming

Lemmings live in the far north. They make long journeys.

leopard

The leopard is a big, strong cat with a spotted coat.

lion

A father lion has a heavy mane.
Other jungle animals are afraid of him.

lizard

A lizard is a kind of reptile.
It has very short legs.

mackerel

Mackerel are ocean fish.
Lots of them swim together.

mammoth

Mammoth was a woolly elephant
of long-ago times.

llama

Llamas live in the high Andes.
They have long, woolly coats.

lobsters

Lobsters live in the sea.
They have strong claws.

loon

Loons dive for fish.

M

minnow

Minnows are small fish.

mole

The mole lives underground.

monkey

Monkeys are the animals
that look most like people.

moose

The moose is a big cousin of the deer.

mosquito

Mosquitoes are insects that often bite people.

mouse

Mice like seeds and cheese. One is a mouse. Two are mice.

N

narwhal

A narwhal is a white whale with a long tusk.

newt

A newt is a small, lizard-like animal that spends part of its life in the water, part on land.

nightingale

A nightingale is a bird that sings very sweetly.

nest

Birds lay eggs in nests.

O

octopus

The octopus has eight arms. It lives on the sea bottom.

opossum

Mother opossum carries babies on her back.

ostrich

The ostrich is a bird that cannot fly. It can run fast.

otter

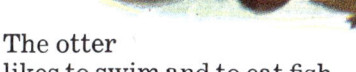

The otter likes to swim and to eat fish.

panda

The panda's home is in far-off Asia.

peacock

The peacock has a very showy tail.

pelican

The pelican has a pouch for holding fish.

penguin

Penguins live near the South Pole. They are birds but they cannot fly.

P

owl

The owl sees best at night.

oyster

Oysters are shellfish that cling to sea rocks.

perch

The perch is a fish that lives in fresh water.

pig

Pigs like to eat. They give us pork and ham and bacon.

pigeon

Many pigeons live in the city.

platypus

The platypus has a duck-like bill and a fur coat. It lays eggs.

polar bear

The polar bear has a thick white coat.

puffin

Puffins are birds that live on the seashore.

prairie dog

The prairie dog is squirrel's cousin. It barks like a little dog.

pupa

A pupa is an insect sleeping in a cocoon.

praying mantis

The mantis eats other insects.

puppy

A puppy is a young dog.

Q

quail

The quail is a plump brown bird.

R

rabbit

A rabbit has long ears and pink eyes.

raccoon

The raccoon hunts food at night.

rat

The rat has a long tail and strong chewing teeth.

reindeer

Reindeer live in the far North.

rhinoceros

The rhinoceros wears a horn on its nose.

rooster

Roosters are father chickens.

reptiles

Reptiles creep or crawl. There are many different kinds.

S

salmon

Salmon swim upstream to lay their eggs.

sandpiper

Sandpipers live along the shore.

sea horse

The sea horse is a strange small fish. It can use its tail like a hand.

seal

Seals are furry sea animals.

sea anemone

Sea anemones are animals which look like flowers.

sea lion

A sea lion is a big seal.

shark

The shark is a swift, fierce fish.

sheep

Sheep have thick coats of wool.

shell

Some sea animals have hard shells instead of bones.

skeleton

A skeleton is made up of bones.

skunk

The skunk can shoot out bad-smelling oil to protect itself.

snail

The snail wears a coiled shell.

snake

Snakes have no legs.
Some snakes can give poisonous bites.

sparrow

Sparrows are common, small birds.

spider

The spider spins a web to catch its food.

sponge

Sponges are soft sea animals.

squirrels

Squirrels live in trees.
They eat nuts.

tadpole

A tadpole is a baby frog.

tail

Many animals have tails behind them.

termite

Termites are insects
that often live in wood.

stork

The long-legged
stork
builds its nest
up high.

sunfish

Most sunfish
are brightly colored
and live in fresh water.

T

tiger

Tigers are big, ferocious cats
with striped coats.

tooth

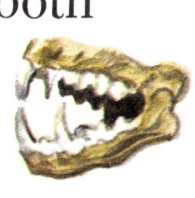 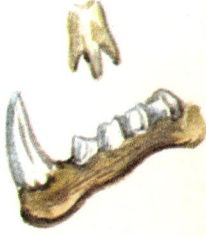

With teeth, animals chew their food.
One is a tooth. Two are teeth.

trout

Trout are beautiful fish.
Fishermen find them hard to catch.

turkey

Turkeys are large birds.
They are good to eat.

turtle

A turtle's bones form its shell.

tusks

Tusks are great, long teeth.

V

vicuña

A vicuña is a shy animal
with fine, soft wool.

vulture

A vulture is a large bird.
It eats dead animals.

W

walkingstick
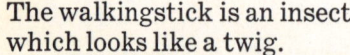
The walkingstick is an insect
which looks like a twig.

walrus
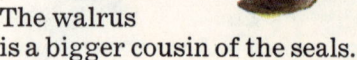
The walrus
is a bigger cousin of the seals.

wasp

Wasps make beautiful nests. Sometimes they sting people.

wolf

The wolf is a swift, wild cousin of the dog.

weasel

The weasel is a small, slim hunter.

woodpecker

The woodpecker finds insects deep inside wood.

whale

The whale is the biggest of all animals.

wing

Birds have wings to help them fly.

worm

Worms are long and round and soft.

Y Z

yak

A yak is a long-haired ox.

zebra

The zebra looks like a small, striped horse.

ZOO

A zoo is a park for animals.
Its full name is Zoological Garden.